TIME OUT OF JOINT

BENEDICT CHIAKA NJOKU

TIME OUT OF JOINT

Selected Poems

THE GOLDEN QUILL PRESS
Publishers
Francestown   New Hampshire

Library of Congress Catalog Card Number 82-84662

ISBN 0-8233-0357-8

Printed in the United States of America

*This volume is dedicated to the late
Madam Maria Elizabeth Ekeoma Njoku, my mother,
who died at a ripe old age of 115 years
in September 1979*

ACKNOWLEDGMENTS

Thanks are due to The Golden Quill Press for publishing this volume; to my secretary, Mrs. Barbara Rayford, and lovely children, Mary Josephine, Bernadette Patricia, Dolores Benedicta and Agatha Rita, for typing the manuscript; to my wife, Mrs. Josephine Njoku, for constantly worrying me to begin to publish the volumes of poetry I have written; to Professor George Ross Ridge for reading the manuscript, and to my Professor, Dr. Craig LaDrière, who introduced me to the world of modern poetry.

CONTENTS

TIME OUT OF JOINT

TO TIME PRESENT: AN ODE

And Time, a seamless web spins on
Until it is no more and glory dawns
And this place of wrath and tears will end
And Time will be no more. There will
Be no more flow, and all Time's urge
To value Time will be no more.

Do we dare to hope for better days?
Our winter wheat brings daily bread
Just something sweet to quench our needs,
To cool our trembling limbs today
While billows howl and tides ebb and flow,
And ne'er ending dreams of lost love
Invade the restless mind of man,
As ceaseless waves beat against the rock.
Or silence, like soft downs, o'er-whelm
This earth of wonders and surprises.

And Time flies over flashing lights
Across verdant fields and sea shores
Soothing discordant impulses
With softer lights and dreamy stars
An endless stream of gems and gifts
From heaven's portal flow for e'er.

It is a short and fragile hour
That stretches from here to other lands
And through the windy paths beyond
A beam of every light and cool air roll

Untouched, unploughed by human hands
A shining light against sand dunes
A brilliant light against cool air.
A lovely rose atop our desks
Is the milk that feed the hungry
Of the world while the rich glut in wealth.

Unwilling to bring sunshine to the poor
Or the world steeped in tragedy
And a thaw on autumn's frosted hills
And summer rose that blooms with grace.

Why all this trouble and bubble!
All this moiling and toiling here!
We moil and toil as our lives double
In Time, with Time, against the Time
This dazzling beams! Abracadabra!
Bubble trouble! Toil and Moil! Life is
A bubble! A fume of smoke in air!

*   *   *

No one can see beyond the crystal sea
A troubled man on an empty sea
Of life half-dazed in blazing light
Like a ship in a bleak and stormy sea.

*   *   *

Is there no tender touch to soothe
A heart diseased, a lonely heart?
A sunshine to light the gloom of day?
A starlit night for happy lovers?

A bed of roses in a sea of troubles?
The hum of bumble bees in soft summer sun?

*   *   *

Our minds are programmed minds
Our thoughts are programmed thoughts
The very home that shelters us
Is robbed of love and care and joy —
What wealth and health cannot give us.
Thus sweet sour airs pervade our airs,
The joyful past has passed away
A dreadful night bears a dreadful sight.

*   *   *

A life of ease and wine and song
Is not our *raison d'être*.
A purposeful life remains our goal.
We buy mistakes and errors all
With mundane wishes that dash our hopes,
And often dazed by dark spells of deemed hate
That is clear to prismic splinters of light.

*   *   *

A world in need, a world in trouble
While waves break against the beach
And willows mourn the passing Time
As sunlight streams through the window panes
To wipe away the misty air
Unfriendly lights in unfriendly nights
When estranged love-lorn youth still mourn
Like broken walls that weep and wail.

*   *   *

The phoenix hovers high and low
And dies only to rise again
The eagle hovers high above
A sunless spotless golden light
To soothe a heart in search of light
A light that beams for those that care
For others' good no matter what.
We are God's children all and all.
And Time past is still present now
While Time present is ours to mend.

I'M LIKE A BUTTERFLY

I am a butterfly as free as air
Veering merrily with the wind.
Flying freely like an untamed fay
Bringing eternal breath to you and me.

I live a timeless life like e'ergreen trees
I sing timeless songs like bards unsung
I sing though there's no place for sainted bards
Who sing of a world blazing newer trails.

My life is for ever and ever
Untrammeled in the seines of Time
Unchained by the shackles of space
Untainted and unpolluted by Time.

My undaunted spirit feels for a world
Where sainted souls are mocked and derided,
A world steeped in confusion and disorder
And trees are shedding their leaves in haste.

I am part of the eternal air
Although my broken limbs hover around
I wheel my trails as I zig-zagly fly
I flutter-flutter with the wind.

I make geometric designs in mid air
And perch gently upon the floral petals
I dodge invading winds and mighty storms
And triumph over the mightiest foes.

I watch the sun peering from the cloud,
And wonder why so much love leads to hate!
And why so much love for fragile things,
Though love will win against hard times always!

I am a spirit sprightly rolling against Time
Immortal wind that flies by day and night
I am stronger than the mightiest oak
Bringing freedom bells that ring for you and me.

TIME PRESENT: A DIRGE

Do not presume to moan and groan the Times!
The past has come and gone. The present reigns.
While the brain drain increases by day and night
And human hearts no longer thaw and glow
The little pattering feet and greedy mouths
Await their day of grace in spite of all
The stormy blasts and hunger spells by day
The rich forget the poor and glut in wealth
They forget the hill through which all must pass.

For far away from here is that river
Flowing through the eddies and shores of life
An empty space across the seas of life
A realm distant, remote, certain and sure
From whose rich bourne and shores no one returns
The wind blowing over the hill reminds
Fragile, fallible man of life's eternal goal
Not joy or sorrow but love sustains all
For love is the balm for man's troubled days
For love carries man through the inevitable hour
That waits for all, the rich and the poor and all.

What soft incense o'er hangs this canopied place!
That tender kiss heralds us to the hill
Each dimpled smile awaits the kiss of death
And life without love is a bubbling stream
That is plagued with meaninglessness
Like eddies new and fresh all life recedes
It comes and goes; it falls to rise again.

And often there's a lull before the storm
In the lull we think of the rose that bloomed
Sometime ago the rose that now has faded
As the river of life continues its unending flow.

The phoenix that hovers high and low
Must die only to rise again to life
The eagle roams in beauty for a while
The dove of innocence caws for renewal
And we are what we are in spite of all
The masks we wear today will not conceal
What we are. The grass that smells so sweet
Will fade one day. The rose of summer day
Will come and go. Its fragrance is buried
In earthen wares. The pride of empty feat
Will fade like foes in early break of day.

The real is a non-real in a world of brains
A motion without laws, is life without grace.
Here probabilities become possibilities!
A sunless spot in a sea of light
A rose among seas of thorns and thistles
An arid spot in a fertile plain
But things must change in a changeless realm
We are Jove's sons, well-loved, and well-cared for.
The birds of silent seas will sing for us
As we wade through marshy paths along the way.

Preserve the tree, the sign of God on earth
Let men on earth Preserve the tree of Time
The Time of life is here. 'Tis time of grace

Releasing mankind trapped like singing birds
And let a gentle breeze arise to soothe
All human pains and breach of faith and love.

I AM A MOULD OF CLAY
FROM THE POTTER'S HANDS

I am a finite man, with wrinkled brows,
The first flock of gray hair invades my head
I care not for these wrinkles and gray hair
These torturing wrinkles bother me not
These locks of grayish hair are no threat to me
I shall not cry or fling myself downwards.

The light of day still blooms with checkered beams
I wade through life, undaunted still, unscared
By human hurt, my light untrimmed, untouched
By soundless storms across the flowing seas
Knowing truly what awaits ahead of me
As I wade through life's stormy shores and waves.

I am a mould of clay from the Potter's Hands
Full of the rich believer's unbelief
And the unbeliever's belief and doubts
Knowing that Death is not the end of all
That it is not a total annihilation
A summer's truth that dampens not our hopes.

In the ebb and flow of deep sea tides I roam,
Watching the daily rhythm of life, the sea waves
In the sunshine of lovely day
Our inner strengths blooming steely anew
Though wisdom fails to conquer frail youth.

I watch myself emerge, unfold, always
Changing, becoming, arriving in being,

Like rosebuds in summer's richest blooms.
A dynamic emergence of daily life
Becomes the real thing, the growth of self
The breath of finite life in a busy world.

I am a mould of clay from my Potter's Hands
I see the light of day bloom from checkered beams
I see those soundless tracks of human trails
As they change from day to day
I seek fresh inner strengths to enflesh myself
For Death is not the end of all for me.

A LOVER'S DREAM

I arise from dreams at night,
Just the early hours of the night,
At the early stirrings and breaths of night.
When the cooling winds are howling.
When bright-starlit foams are shining
And star-crossed lovers are groaning.

I arise from dreams at night,
To count my blessings by star-light,
To see if I can to some in gloom bring light;
I arise on my feet to bless the fate
That leads my spirit straight to thee,
To make the old transformed anew.

I arise from dreams at night,
I gaze at twinkling stars by night,
Or else breathe sweet gloomy air at night;
I peep and peer through the air at night
Eager to steal a kiss from whom I love
Or lose myself in a daze for my love.

I arise from dreams at night,
The lingering air oozes through the night,
Or filters through my door at night;
But sweet are the thoughts that linger
Hauntingly like the nightingale's dirge
In the weird hours of the night.

I arise from dreams at night,
To seek new life at the sweep of night,

Or lift myself from the stench of night,
To save the sinking ship of state
Or else perish with it and lose my pride;
I'll lift my inner self to raise new hopes.

I arise from dreams at night,
To steal some kisses from her at night
Ere the moon hides herself at night.
Let my love shine in your breast tonight!
While my heart beats with loving fear of thee,
Just press your breast to mine fore'er.

LET THE HEAVENS OPEN
TO RAIN DOWN PEACE

My soul enthralled like spears of summer grass
Upon the meadowstrip across our fields
There hear the moan of doves among the trees
And the soft murmuring of humming bees
How sad and sweet to me are all life's beams!

To the dead a deathless hour pervades the realm
Upon the lovely moon we fix our eyes
As our yellow years in the full flush of youth
The bugle calls have taken a heavy toll
How strange in mood and mould this mortal world!

I can still hear echoes of a world sweet and sour
The blast of trumpet, the lowing herd and bird songs
The jumbo jet that creaks and whines on trails
These mellow sounds in a sea of glory
Have given us a sparkling lease of life.

So let the heavens open to rain down peace
To us half shrunk like autumn leaves, all pale
And wan and scattered by gusts of human ills.
We have all withered like tender shoots at noon!
Oh rip apart the starry dome! Bring PEACE!

WHAT IS MY NAME

My Name is Jesus
   A sea of tears gush through my weepy eyes
As I hang loosely on the cross
   Bearing my crown of thorns
And my sea of wounds bleeding all over.

I am standing between two thieves
   And Mary, my mother,
And Mary Magdalene and John,
   My Brother, were all there!

Here I stand, once a babe
   Chubby with damask cheeks
Frolicking like winter frogs,
   Climbing, and hugging mother dear.

But now, I'm bereft of joy
   Mourning in grief
As they cast lots on my garments
   And slap my lacerated limbs.

O come and mourn with me
   You passers-by!
The darkening clouds and the silvery drops
   Will bring joy to you.

THE ROOTS ARE FULL OF SAP

The radiant gleam of noonday sun reveals
That day dreams fade as petals fade at noon,
Cool air from pools of inland Springs invade
The countryside to cool some thirsty throats
Or rouse fragile hearts in fragile frames.

But hope for better life enkindled remain
The goal of life amid soothing night air
There are no cruel flames to dim the light
Of faith that burns with glowing sparks and beams
But only songs to light the burden of life.

The earth itself bristles, its dazzling gleams
Bring life from naked trees which blossom forth
With memories that lurk in the bosom of man,
And life begins to bloom with intermittent spurts
Like beams of light that bring strings of delight.

The roots are full of sap, the flowers fair,
All Nature blossoms forth in wild ecstasy
All life's highways are scattered with beauty,
Behold! A sight that brings relief to all!
And brings that flaming fire of love to all.

The sparks of love begin to spread their wings
To bless the earth with warmth and flames of fire
And man begins to mend the crooked paths
That love like golden dreams brings sunlit streams
And gleaming morning dew to you and me.

I HAVE A SONG TO SING

I have a song of sunset air to sing
Of seas of apple blossoms rich and ripe
When lovely roses unfold in beauty rare
A soothing song against a warning moon.
The moon that glows in silvery mists awaits
The song I sing from Eastern vales beyond.

There is no way to hide a broken heart
No way to ride roughshod the Western Hills
The rustling winds at dawn will bring a touch
Of love to human hearts o'er wrought with hate
The bitter sweet of songs both sweet and sad
The soaring eagle pauses to take its breath.

The city lights that flicker at dawn
Throw light on empty faces, bald heads that shine
On sleepy eyes and freckled cheeks at dawn
I know no dark and stormy nights, no hate
In God's abode on earth. No ugly look
On earthen men who bear the grace of God.

A stifled breath and muffled sneeze can not
Restrain a touch of flu and creeping night.
All cosmic beauty fades like breath of air
These mountain crags and peaks of heat at dawn
Can melt the dreams and hopes as yet unborn
And bring relief and gifts to hearts of gold.

These ripples stir a peaceful sea of love
To soothe a heart alone beside the waves,

The poet's songs at dawn will calm the waves
And bring cool breeze to cool the noon day sun
And cloudless skies to shroud the gloom of pain
And priceless gift of grace to man below.

MY FLOWER VASE

I bought a flower vase to plant my rose
I came to a spot in the fields of Texas
To plant my rose where the flag was fluttering
Like singing birds flapping their wide wings by day
Amidst whistling winds and rustling leaves
And here I set my vase on a hill to grow.

And soon it blossomed forth with life and grace
And brought forth new life among the prairies
And now my plant is growing in strength and form
Its beauty sure and exquisite in all the world
It took command of all the world around
Bringing quiet peace and love and joy to all.

Today it blooms like the Eastern star that shines
In beauty non-descript in human words
With purple patches of changes, charges and challenges
As Nature showers her gifts and graces on earth
And joy among the beasts and birds and bushes
And rich aroma and fragrance and sweet smell.

In a world of dazzling and fading beauty
In a mythless, flashy world of things on wings
There is the star that sustains and maintains all things
That cools all heated frozen hearts of men
That brings a comely air that soothes bleeding wounds
And binds all human hearts and heads to peace on earth.

MARANA THA

The gilded clouds are spreading low their wings
As now my gazing soul begins to dwell
In awe and fear against earth's gilded lights
From heaven's doors to light beclouded hearts,
Behold the Root of Life, the Source of grace!

Here purple plums and apple blooms begin
To spread sweet smiles and smells on gilded hearts
While apple boughs begin to bow in awe
Overwhelming the earth with cooling winds
And refreshing airs in joyous mood. Behold!

My hopeful fancy falls on restful hearts
The willow weeps, the orchid sleeps for joy
As lordly Nature poises for a joyous Birth
A radiant star sends forth its shining beam
And never more will life be the same on earth.

Behold now Beauty creeps from gilded clouds!
The cooing doves excite the longing earth
The cuckoo flaps her wings in exultation!
The market stalls and toilet walls are clean;
All creatures pause to hail the King of Kings.

The Lord of Might, the Rod of Jesse has come;
The Key of David's line, the King of Kings!
The Rising Sun, the Wisdom from on High!
Awake! Ye men of God; The King of Kings
Is here. Let's spread the holly wings! Awake!

Marana Tha! Marana Tha! Come Lord!
Venez, mon Dieu!   Venez mon Dieu!   Venez!
Viene Dio mio!   Viene, Dio mio!
Venid, Señor!   Venid Señor!   Venid!
Bia Onyenweanyi ni!   Bia!

THE ETERNAL DAWN

The sun that sets westward
Proclaims another day
The sun's repose becomes
A birth for other realms
It hides from mortal view
What God has made for all
While life is passing on.

A gentle touch of God
From heaven's gate to man
And what appears a repose
Becomes another day
A dawn that brings new life
Of love and ease and care
No trial of faith for man.

But yes, a trial of hope
And strength and care and joy
With sweeter care and joy
A life of love and grace
That makes all men like God
In soul and spirit all
The sun that sits will rise.

THERE IS NO SWEETER JOY

There is no sweeter joy
There is no sweeter sound
Than one in troubled times
When days seem dark and black
And hope begins to fail
And love begins to fade.

Tis better than robed kings
And mitered kings in robes
And sways of ancient kings
There is joy in sorrow
And joy in perfection
A perfect blend of love.

Earth's shadows begin to lengthen
As work begins to wear
The seal of Jesus Christ
Who came to heal our wounds
To heal our broken bones
For behold He's here today!

There is no sweeter sound
Than the chorus from heaven
There is no greater care
Than the loving care
Of Him who in joy said:
"Behold I am with you always."

THE SIRENS MIDNIGHT SONG

Let's go now Brother mine,
No more your "Festina lente,"
Before the world is sealed with blood
Confused! Derobed! Like a dying man.
Deflated like old tubes! Desouled! Apathetic!
Dehumanized! Detached! Deformed! Dissolved!

Let's go now Brother mine,
In flannel suits, gabardines and mohair.
Before the Blindfold game is over;
We have long played Okwe. 'Tis game of chance.
Our morning tea outbids the noon tea with sweets.
The Black tipped drum looms like tingling strings.

Let's go before the morning tea and English muffins
Let's go, we tarry much. Let's go, we wait too long
Like noon tides struggling beneath a silent sea.
While dizzy prudes at bay nudely peep out
Of window panes, seeking the light of the day.

Let's go now Brother mine,
If Fait chaud. Tempus fugit!
Let's go while time and tide are ripe
Nemo dat quod non habet.
Let's go before the oppressor triumphs
In human butchery. Arms don't make a man!
Away from the realm where murder is pride
Where killing is treated with impudent mesmerism.
Where guns and bombs are adored and worshipped.
Away from smoking oven tops and perfumed fire places.

Let's go to make our case, to sing our songs.
"While the wind of change" stills into our rooms.
Let's go to bring the world to senses. Awake.
    Marchons. Vite!
We must release our love. We must bring out our hearts
Souled, masculine, compassionate, Reasonable!
The wigged beauty smiles; the poor blasé.
The rich glut in wealth and boast of strength.
The pound weeps, the Dollar slips, the Frank sleeps
The Mark reaps, the yen flaps its wings.
And eagles boast of strength untold.
Superficial is the glamour of wealth and power!

Let's go to the land with many isles of peace,
To bring a bit of love to worlds of hate,
Let's go where we may sing our songs of peace and love,
In spite of giants' roar and raging storms of war,
I hear they pile mounds of deadly fire power.
While still drinking tea together and wallowing
With coffee pots brewed on smoky ovens.

Let's go now Brother mine
Detached! Determined! Prepared to die!
Let's go as eagles of peace with silent trumpets.
Away from tea and toast and cakes and ice cream soda.
Let's go to quench the thirst for conquest.
To soothe the roaring tiger and calm human tenseness.
There's time for everything; Time to sleep; Time to eat;
Time to wake and Time to think of the warp and woof of
    life
And "Time for you and time for me."
And time for bags of food to fill the hungry world.

And time to stop this murderous spree in our southlands,
And time to bring Christ back to the world.

Let's go away from sameness and loneliness,
From tea and toast and tea with cream,
From pots of coffee pods and hot dog feasts,
From cookouts on rainy days,
From masks of reality and increasing gloom,
From tingling strings to booming drums,
From bacon and egg and pancakes for petit diner.

Let's go now Brother mine,
While the soldiers still come and go. Invading
Our innocent victims. Heaving curses on the poor,
And butchering the poor and the helpless breeds
Let's go to regain our lands while the searchers run,
Let's go to stop blood-thirsty foes
While the dead spirit of Rhodes helps our cause
What's the use of this ceaseless carnage!

Let's go now Brother mine,
Let's take the olive branch and *Omu* to seek peace
Let's go to stop Kruger's pride and impending blood baths
Let's pacify the irate few and mollify their threats.
Let's make the way for our African Dream.

Let's go Brother mine,
While the sirens sing their songs that seduce,
Like cracked cornets at midnight,
Along deep sea waves and threatening storms,
While fortune treads and traces its rough paths
Like young babes estranged from mothers' wombs.

Let's go and tarry no longer,
Let's go to stop these senseless killings
In our sun-bathed shores and sun-roasted lands,
Let's go to heal the Fisher King,
To bring clean water now to these thirsty shores.

Let's go, Brother mine,
Let's go right now to sing,
"Let there be peace on earth
And let it begin with me."
Shalom! O-O-O-O-O-O-! Shalom!

A JOURNEY TO THE SOUTHLANDS

A hot and humid sweltering noon it was;
A hotter day you never had;
Yet not so hot as to stop our journey south.
The roads were crooked and winding,
With thorns and thistles to shock a traveller.

It was the heat of summer day;
The sea shady, calm and still and stuffed with fish.
The air was rarefied and relentlessly tumid.
Our travellers, from far off lands came in droves of threes
Eager, determined, blood thirsty, appalled!
Untouched by the souring waves of heat,
Nor by the sun-roasted paths and lanes,
Nor by the air polluted by pride and fortune's frail forces,
Nor by the hidden foes brandishing their heavy steels,
And Nature was friendly, concerned and Empathetic!

The one bore a Rose of Peace
The other a lovely Olive Branch of Peace,
The third bore *"l'eau de Paris"* of Peace,
And a halo emitting intermittent flashes of lights.

Down and down in the humid air and foaming heat,
Across endless tracks of land, air and sea,
All determined, courageous and devout!
Onward through thick and thin, through rain or drought.
Like pilgrims embarked on a holy trek to Aro Chukwu,
Or like crusaders when ages were dark and dim.

Onward and down and down all dreary and dry,
Like a trek to a dry, infertile realm of gold,
Our men were weary and wary with the crush
Of wars undeclared, yet fought with ferocity unknown,
All determined to save the dying from Death's dead
    Kingdom.

In a room Madame Bovary was luring her preys,
And Fraulein Muller was casting her spell
On lusty fools, cursing fate and saintly life;
And old Sir Falstaff was quaffing in noon droughts,
And youthful blokes were groping at the miniskirts,
Half dazed with wine, women and song,
Unmindful yet of Death's inevitable doom.

And pointing their fists against the lure of grace,
And looking askance at any threat of grace;
And lights were burnt out, their lives dreary and dim,
And straddling the fence and walking the thin line
Between good and evil while forces of history gathered
    together
A harder time there never was — An unthinking time!

At the other end there was a group, a non-descript,
Slouching through life half sleep, tense and dazed.
A harder time there never was,
Suffused with uncertain outcome,
And like the Quest for the Holy Grail, we went
With snatches of joy and sorrow,
Pious of intent, devout in design
Prayerful in execution, doleful and daring
Donna Nobis Pacem.

Soon we came to the Doldrums, a calm windless strand
Dull, dreary a dreary; Only the daring could proceed
"Dulce et Decorum Pro Patria Mori"
The Palace Perilous adjoined the strand
The Quester's paradise with mild and welcome air.
A hotter realm was never imaginable!
The forest was dense with tangled undergrowth,
A Black eagle faced a white vulture
Both ogled each other as from colored spectacles.

At the Presidential where old and modern cultures
    interplay
There was a shock of sameness. Of tea and toast and cake,
Of miniskirted blondes and brunettes,
Of gabardine suits and flannel suits,
The black eagle strumming the piano. Crescendo!
The white and black keys beamed with harmony
Orchestrating the peace that the travellers sought.
Shalom! Shalom! "Udo": "Pax Christi."

The monkey strolled across the garden,
Gibbering in audible notes in rapid succession.
The air was filled with confusion. A Babel!
As ladies poured in wearing halters, tank tops,
Mid-drifts, and tube tops and blue jeans, dancing
The "bump," the "hustle," the "White Boy," the Boogie
    fever."
The "roller coaster." No traditional steps!
The booming drum still loomed over the air
Shalom! "Udo!" "Pax Christi." "Donna Nobis Pacem."

And many meters of journey remained,
To the land of the Rhodes and the Searches for wealth.
Where human greed had produced vast human carnage
Where the cities were vast human shambles
There life was cheap, derobed of sense, soulless.
Where human voices remained silent.
Where world bodies shilly shallied the proper course
To pacify man's insatiable desires for worldly goods.

There we were; the evening air was crisp,
The meadows gay; too gay to be war-torn,
The orchards lush with juicy oranges and banana fruits.
War weary soldiers craved for peace
Madam Igolo, the Single Rose in a jungle of thorny bush,
Threw her charms to lull all to sleep,
A sleep of peace to soothe broken hearts
And balm all wounds. In a heap of cactus
Red roses grow. The good performed the task
Of shock blocks or serve as think tanks
In a thoughtless world. Here we must sleep.

Through wastelands and oasis we have travelled
Across the "Slough of Despond," through mire and marsh
Now weary and tired. The journey long and tedious
"Let there be peace on earth."
In spite of greed, let's move together as friends.
"Udo!" *"Pax vobis cum,"* a voice said.
"Udo!" *"Donna nobis pacem."* Amen! another replied.
The world is wide enough for all. *Udo!   Udo!*
O! O! O! O! O! O! O!

THE HARMATTAN OF HUMAN LIFE

It is midnight and Our Lady's Church Bell
And Assumpta Bell chime with booming sounds
Around my room, resounding with deep echoes.
A strain of gloomy music filters through
My ears, like strange, stray chords at witches eve
While ardent lovers groan in awe and misty breaths.

Beyond these strange seas cool tombs moan and groan
O'er the mute, sad, silent memories of the Dead,
Like the cool of spent emotions in life's aches
And pains, whole nightly ghosts make their nightly rounds.
The whispering pine with mingled frowns sings strains
And chords of gloom and doom, of down-trodden man.

I need a batch of joy to rouse saddened hearts;
The falling leaves endear the trees to us;
I am afraid of Death but cannot force
The issue. Tea cups and marmalade have their charms;
Below the Millkin Hills are tales of Fortune's frowns
In graves that bemoan the Fall of Princes.

Beside the molten earth and groves of golden leaves
And aching, trembling hands and the North East winds,
And the lights of day crashing into cold ridden nights,
And a world of dead and dying woods and strange moods,
And the world that broods in gloom like spent grooms,
Our golden oil still oozes from deep crevices.

Cool winds disperse cold chills as dawn pierces the skies
And strips of grief whittle away without relief.
Sea water coils to curl again with warm curls,
And sea waves trembling in floating air calm down,
The clouded mirror drains its fog in sun light;
There's room to move upward despite staggering odds.

These thoughts have haunting air-strange, strangled and
    chilly!
But misty fields of yam dispel the wave
Of myth, only to face a holy air
Of mystery and charm that looms anew
Where juicy oranges vie with pungent grapefruits
To hail the solemn hush of Christmas Eve.

It was a silent hush to hail the King of Kings
And hail the Light to kindle the darkness of years.
And now alone or in groups mute voices resound with new
    notes
Despite strange tales of littering leaves and falling life.
A flock of birds are hovering in mid-air
With wings outward in prayerful mood to hail Him.

The robin sweeps across the air with flapping wings
Upward, downward, in smooth sailing mood
Like roller skates it zig-zags its sprite way
Across our skies it swoops and sweeps and reels.
A welcome sight to calm disturbed mankind
Steeped deeply in life of human senses and pride.

I have sailed through strange seas and pains of thought
I have seen the trees in their Harmattan beauty show,
I have shed tears of love and tears of pain,
I have seen the fallen leaves derobing
Our lovely trees. I have seen that the sea never dries.
I know that He has come to save the world.

ONLY LOVE CAN TAME THE BIG LIONS

When two mighty lions roar the world quivers
Each lovely creature boasts of its might
Each finds pleasure in arm twisting and sabre rattling.
They brag of wealth and martial might
While a troubled world sits and waits for peace.

Each lion has a stockpile of destructive weaponry,
The use of which can only fan the chord of discord:
And ignite their flaming swords and popping guns,
When mankind languishes in uncertainty.
Until man recognizes the mighty hands of God.

Until mankind knows once and for all
That cold or hot war, psychic or physical war
Is inimical to the cause of brotherly love.
The blinding fumes of fire power do not make life more
    worthy.
Victory in war is but a passing fad.

For a war soon won is soon forgotten.
The inner fumes that lead to war
Are born of illusions of grandeur
Time and love are healers of wounds
And love abides where peace resides.

In the cozy bosom of peace is love
The fleeting joys of relentless gunnery
Are but passing moments in human life.
A war soon won soon moves into oblivion,
And thinking man is haunted by remorse.

The world must not yield to the pressure for war
Let the world pacify the warring lions
Let the world offer them a loving heart
Let the world offer them listening ears.
Nemo est judex in sua causa.

A world divided is a world weakened;
A world in two camps is courting disaster,
Courting death by fire, wallowing in battle,
Courting blood baths, swimming in blood,
Courting manslaughter, spitting human blood.

But peace is the goal of all thinking men,
A peace built firmly on freedom and love,
A peace which acts as beacon light for men
A peace which prowls the profundities of life
A peace which acts like cool drinks on warm days.

I'VE WALKED WITH THE POOR

I've been with them before, I've walked with them
Whose grass is never green, whose luck is hard;
I've groaned with them, I've moaned with them, the
   Poor!
Who sigh with grief in the heyday of wealth and health
I've grieved with them, I've walked with them at night.

And here again they are, distant and strange
Transformed, Transfused, Transgressed, Transmuted,
Unwined, undined, Unclad and saddened with grief,
Once more I see distant blazing fire.
Of rancour, and discontent, overwhelming the world.

Amid the clatter and chatter of evening meals
I see consuming fire at heat of day. Unquenchable!
A world betrayed is a world delayed;
I see food power, fertilizer power
And oil power race to a collision course.

A world, unsafe, betrayed, retrenched is born
And like a mysterious creature it hustles for a place.
We are enclosed in a madhouse full
Of insecurities, at the brink of fire.
And gloomy outlook o'erwhelms our resolve.

I see a woeful wind in a grove of fruits.
I see a world of bleakness for the poor
As others in wealth and health bathe themselves.
The Poor also want to reach the "Promised Land"
Of health and wealth whose souls are Doves of Peace.

The world is like a bride and a groom who strive
To mesh the microgrooves of their personalities
Or like a middle-aged man who pales
Beside a threat of Death from source unknown.
We glut in wealth and dance with Death unknown.

To differ can be fun. To vary may provide
A spice to life for newly weds at prime,
Who want a spark of light to grace their lives.
To mouth the norms of dove-like life may check
The threat to holy life and indifference.

I see the earth a launching pad for life of peace.
We must expose ourselves to the crude realities
Of our world, the sad inequities of fortune
Where the poor are crushed by hunger and want
By woes of wants and pressing needs in times of plenty.

And now, my friend, let's help the the poor, the weak
While honest labor grooms its gifts of grace
While the peanut farmer strives to feed the rich
Whose fingers are ringed with precious gems of gold.
Like glittering, shimmering pearls on ocean deep.

The harmattan comes with groves of luscious fruits
A spell of mellow winds to lull us to downy sleep.
To bring the poor to realms of wealth and health
To melt strange seas and mists of thought which float
Like waves in fading air, now drooping, now swaying.

We are menaced by monsters of gold and poor
We must avoid the daring fear of loss
Which baffles an age of greed and wealth
Where Eagle vies with Gold and Dove of Peace
I've walked with the Poor on whom Fortune frowns.

I've walked with the Poor, I'll love the Poor on earth!
C'est la vie. What lives must die. What dies still lives
And Time is a healer sure and supreme
And Time soon drifts into timeless realms of gold.
I've walked with the Poor! I'll help the Poor.

IF WISHES WERE HORSES

If wishes were horses, poor men would ride;
If wishes were dreams, poor men would dream;
If I were time, I'd have enough of Me
To do what I would like to do.

If I retained the World of Time,
To do the things I want to do,
I'd fill the world with songs and love,
To ease the pain of hate on earth.

I'd pluck a bouquet of roses,
To fume the world with song of love;
I'd ask the Source of life and Time;
To make my life a joy to you.

If I had a box of wishes
I'd fill it with thought of you;
If wishes control the rhythm of life
I'd dance the tunes that chime with love.

But wishes are not of dreams or Time,
Nor is there enough of Time to dream
Away the charms of life on earth
Where lovers moan, and haters groan.

I'M AN AFRICAN

I'm an African, born free,
As free as air; With spirit free
To move the path of life,
Unmoved by waves and storms.

I'd rather be me, black as jet,
Brown of eyes. A heavy head
On a fragile body, unencumbered
And sure of His reward for me.

I'm an African, a man from a strange land
Of strange people. A people in a hurry
To arrest the tide of Time,
Eager to be, to do, and love.

I'd rather be me, brown as berry,
With an aura of hope for better things to come,
A freshness that charms, a rhythm fresh,
When the going is hard. I am an African.

THE MASKS I WEAR

I wear the mask of a work-a-holy man
With spectacles on my nose I wade my way;
I am afraid that people may not accept me as I am,
I am ashamed to be what'er I am.

I wear the mask of Christ whose Cross I bear;
With deceptive pose I waltz my way on earth;
I am afraid to be real and true,
Or else I may lose my cherished esteem.

I wear the mask of a busy man, working,
A manly pose that looks for love and care
The man of grace and love and jolly mood
For whom this life has served with joy and care.

I wear the mask of a cheerful man, smiling,
While deep in me the devil lurks around;
I am afraid to take a stand to be counted,
For fear I might escape an accolade.

I wear the mask of manly men, afraid of none,
While my inner feeling breathes mistrust and hate,
In angry tone I hide my fearful pose,
And show myself as a model pure and simple.

I *wear* the *mask* of a *loving man*, loving;
The garb of a happy man, a man of grace,
Yet I am insensitive to others' feelings
Because I think the sea will never dry.

O dear! grace still like wild geese, chases me around,
It lurks not around the corner gate;
I must face the facts of life without a break,
For I have friends to win and walls to mend.

THERE'S NO NEED FOR GREED
AND CARELESS CARE

She stumbles suddenly over the hill and stoops,
While panting fast with breath; she clings to her wheels
A jar of homogenized milk spilling over the vale,
With zippered evening shades, her lips trembling
With awe, her breath now hot with fume and fury.

Weary a-weary she stops, her wig tangled on her spokes,
Half blown away by a restless sandy storm —
Vulnerable to draughts of merciless air from heaven's realm,
She foams and grunts with ire, her cozy breath failing,
And earth was deaf to self inflicted pain!

The evening moon still hangs heavy on slippered glory
Above the astral beauty the heavens dance her glory,
Clustered in yellow leaves the checkered horizon,
Blinking with brilliant lights that charm the earth,
While Mother Nature snores with measured joy.

The heavens hug the spotted earth whose shutters open
To hide the melting airs from stormy winds
And everything thrills below the sharp-edged scarlet hills
While dappled glory shocks the world around
As biting, baffling winds overcharge the air.

She stands aghast, while the howling winds still roar
Like howling wolves they shake the earth like tremor,
Emitting belching smoke from Mother earth
Thick endless smoke that dazes the eye
While twilight creeps above the star-tipped fields.

Soon a soft welcome wind comes to calm the earth,
While bush fowls cackle in the fallow fields
Beyond the creeping dust and shattered dreams,
To say: "The world is good for all of us
And there's no need for greed and careless care."

BEWARE OF HOUSES
WITHOUT THE HOMELY GRACES

Who breathes anew those melodic airs of yore? —
He who on nature's wings strums the Aeolian harp.
To sing those merry songs that charm like the air —
He who with merry notes uplifts the senses
To rouse the world to drink melodic air —
A hungry heart that soothes the burdened hearts.

The power of the minstrel's lyre conjures us all;
And wakes the dizzy sleep of drier nights,
While Venus roams among the lilies red,
His charmed airs like incense pollute the air,
While bright lights from heaven's gate awake
The sleepy grooms o'erwhelmed with lover's wine.

The bitter care and bitter fruits of life
Can mould a heart that swims with bitter pills.
Beneath those starry isles lurk the lover's nest;
And surer hearts in lover's paradise
Will melt the reign of hate in human hearts,
And drive away the monstrous monster of Sin.

Above, half moon, the setting sun is gone,
To rouse the snoring day, the tangled woods,
While sleeping men are faint with wounds and stings
Their battle lines are soaked with blood and wounds
Of men unsung, unknown, their banners worn
With age, and rage, the scourge of bloody wars.

The Pelican that nestles atop our roof,
A pearl, a brightening shade on wintry night,
The swan dares wade upon the flood of blood
The spills upon our land, like debris of time,
To crush the bloated prose, the murky verse,
The ruins our search for love, and care, and truth.

Sweet Pelican that heals and feeds with blood,
That flows from His side, the Sacred Wounds
Bring Heaven's light to light our darkened shores,
Suffused with cunning faces that wear a smile —
Those smiling faces that lure the virgin to death.
Beware of houses without the homely graces!

INFLATION

Trance-like, he stands and speechless, wary!
Aghast, indeed shaken by recession and depression!
And inflation! Wary, weary, a-weary!

Inflation and Depression! Yes, inflation!
But more so: Deprivation and nostalgia,
For want of values that matter!

And depression at loss of worthwhile values!
And inflation of human desires and needs!
And inflation of human expectations!

We are content and filled with life's "goodies"!
Content with and inflated by life's sustaining things,
That don't placate life's insatiable desires!

The more we have, the more our needs inflate!
And trains and chains of needs our path inflate!
Expand, distend, like troops in a battle line!

And like avalanche our things distend!
Life's deeper notes begin to illude the earth
As lifeless things become our goal on earth!

Filled with things, let us deflate, retrace our steps!
To follow the footpath of Him who Is —
Jesus yesterday, today and forever.

He was depressed into our servile state,
Deflating His Kingly state to a slave's,
His virgin Birth to satisfy our human needs!

Come friends, deflate, and be deflated of Thingdom!
And be emptied of things and selfish, self love,
That war against His kingdom of love!

Be filled with love that lasts, the love of Him!
For God is love and love abides in Him,
Whose Way does not inflate and is not inflated.

THE ENERGIES OF YOUTH

With the optimism of youth
Dark doubts in life will melt away
And give way to the light of day
For youth is joy, love and peace
Unspoiled by unbroken praise and the waves
Whose eddies ripple with joy and love.

Here life pulsates with the force of youth
Always searching and striving with rigor
With gleams of hope in his dark blue eyes
He faces the massive problem of life with vigor,
Throwing his energies into the struggle
Against the vicious cycle of poverty and want.

He digs parched and waterless grounds
In search of water from the deep seas
Until water gushes from flinty rocks
To quench human thirst for justice and truth
The ocean deeps abound with waters of joy
As the blue skies above in glory sing.

The earth abounds with untold heaps of joy
The morning stars begin to glow
As daily music resounds the glory of heavens.
Who made the heavens high and great?
Who gave the birds their sweet songs of joy?
Who made the water lilies, the larks and all?

O what fools we mortals are!
How concealed the flashing seas remain!

If we not open our eyes to light and love
Loveliness evaporates with strife and hate
But a love response fills the earth with joy
Let us therefore with heart and mind respond.

TIME

Of Time, the mighty Time, the endless flux I speak.
Of Time, just now and time after.
And there is Time for you and Time for me.
And Time for everything, For lover's song
The Time that heals the heartaches and shocks of life.
The Time that raises the dark shades of hate
And lightens the heavy and weary weight of life.
The Time that airs itself in song of praise —
There is a Time for joy and a Time for tears!
    A Time for love, and a Time for hate!
    A Time for war, and a Time for peace!
    A Time for life, and a Time for death!
    A Time for mother and a Time for father!
There is a Time to love, and a Time to think!
    A Time to kneel, and a Time to heal!
    A Time to plant, and a Time to reap!
    A Time to take, and a Time to give!
    A Time to come, and a Time to go!
    A Time to gain, and a Time to lose!
    A Time to speak, and a Time to be silent!
O Time, Thou spark of eternity! Irrevocable Time!
O Time! the mighty Time, You toil and moil!
And roll and roll and roll and roll! in Time!
You pass o'er the flux of day and night!
Move on, Timeless Time, the balm of wounds!
Your here and now must matter much!
Your continuous process of aging baffles me!
O Lord, let me spend my rolling Time in love of you!
Let there be a scourge on the hand of hate.
I will not be a slave to Time on earth.

WHAT ARE COLOR STROKES?

Your color strokes, your views are sometimes clear
And sometimes warped, call yourself what you may.
You are somebody too, a jewel bright and clear;
A golden lock in a blooming garden.

You stand forever tall in this garden of life.
A glint in your eyes is bright like gold.
You drive away blotched; tainted shades of pale
To warm the earth with color gay and bright.

Don't dare to drag the drab green of greed
O'er your cool head, for you are somebody dear.
You warm the earth with a burst of smiles.
You make me feel warm and glad to live.

Be not the man with ego shattered
In the fragmented dust of life, the nobodies
In a world of "somebodies," the "put-downs"
With nobody to praise. Be somebody now!

FACING THE MISSISSIPPI

Dark, blue the gentle river roars
Like a mighty ocean
Separating immense land mass.
Time moves, wades gently
Gives and takes back at the same time.
Breathes in and out,
Shrinks, strikes,
Gathers and scatters,
Roams and moans,
The waves ebb and flow
In little eddies
Splashes, widens again!

The summer plunges
Enjoys and regrets;
The recession and inflation
Of the waves of time,
The inflation and depression
Which impose impotence in all —
The rich and the poor,
Finite and infinite,
To be born is to die!
To live is death
When everything is topsy-turvy
Integrity is on trial!

To remain in the water!
To dive for a mile!
To move on and not return!

To be and not to be!
Simple existence in essence!
To be one: The silent majority!
Oh-where is the abode of thought?
There will be time. Other Times
"But rise! Rise! Lo 'tis Time."

Against the Disorder of times!
Against purposeless impudence!
Against the shock of time!
To win or lose is not the goal.
To be transformed to self!
To be onesself and not another!
That's the test of life!
To be myself just as I am! This is life.

Away! Away! From the blue vaults of the sky
Masquerading as Joe and Jean.
That's not a noble act!

THE DANCER

The mighty Drum, like thunder roars,
And while the drum rumbles, the dancer fumbles,
And like heaps of leaves amidst the ripples of rain,
The dancer steps like one who lusts for gold in days of old.

Forward and backward the dancer rolls
With a bundle of roses in poses he holds his own,
For love and roses are one and grow in poses.
And so with roses and poses the dancer in beauty rolls.

With measured steps the dancer walks,
While the drum rumbles and rumbles,
Like one in love with life and jolly good time,
And gently down and down he stoops with rhythm.

Forward and backward like gentle breeze he swings,
His hands stretch to heavenwards with sweet repose;
For though life is sweet, heaven is sweeter still,
The dancer swings his head heavenward for peace.

Like the ship of life, he sets sail to the tune of music,
And ploughs at dawn from day to day;
Upwards and downwards he trots in beauty
Like rose of May which blooms with radiance.

Downwards and upwards the dancer steps
To bring his gift of love and beauty to all,
To melt frozen hearts with beams of hope,
Or with radiant colors to adorn the earth.

The mighty Drum rumbles like silent thunder,
While the dancer sways upwards and downwards,
And round and round in a merry-go-round,
With swollen hearts and controlled breath.

Up and down, forward and backward he twists,
And rolls like voluble piece of gum;
Smoothly, smoothly and smoothly he sways,
With hope to spray the earth with love and peace.

I AM A CATERPILLAR

I am a caterpillar filled with leaves
All green around I sing my song
Half dazed with sleep, I cannot see
The Light Green as grass, I wear fine thread
Spun all around, fettered to the leaf.

Here I am weaving around myself
Closing myself all around, shuttling
Like an engine, drowsy, deaf and dumb
Dreaming of my tomorrow, unsure!
Shall I wither and decay?

Green as grass, hidden from view
With hue indistinguishable!
Only half remembered by puffs of air
Quivering among green leaves
Spinning myself round and round!

Soon I begin to grow huge eyes
Rough hued all around, from head to toe,
With tasty mouths, long legs and fleshy hands
And wings with rings and plumes of gold.
Creeping into life as the lovely sun was shining.

And soon my wet short wings begin to open
My dazzling eyes begin to see around
And my wide open mouth begins to gape
For food, and love, and ease and breath of air.
And my veins begin to open and here I am.

I am a caterpillar, a budding life on earth
A bunch of veins, and wings and rings and eyes.
I can dance and lance and jostle too.
I twist my eyes and bend my wings
Always rising, creeping and flying.

I AM NOT READY TO DIE

I am not ready to die today
No I am unready for I've some kinks
Some kinks in my mien
No I'd prefer the lonely exile here
The constant wonder and mystery of life of earth.

I am not ready to die today
Until all kinks are wiped from me
I have a zest for life,
With ever-deepening love for life
With enthusiasm and joy for life.

I am not ready to die today
In spite of overwhelming odds
I'm willing to stay longer here
Here in this vale of tears
With its thorns and thistles.

I am not ready to die today
In spite of heavy odds
I'd rather stay on more on earth
With its sweat and tears
With its storms and stresses.

I am not ready to die today
I'd rather live longer in this beautiful garden
With miles and miles of desert lands
And a world of tangled jungles
In man's life in this temporary home.

The earth is still a joyous place to live
It's a beautiful garden with some weeds
It's a tingling and thrilling place
A place of fascination and charm
A place to erase the strains of life.

I will use my gift of time
In spite of crushing weight of earthly life
I shall use my gift of heart and mind
Until eternity claims me
When my journey is done.

Truly I am not ready to die today
Here I shall enjoy the flowers which bloom and die
And the birds which sing, the fishes that swim
I shall not be ready to die
Until heavenwards I am ready to wade.

A PAEAN TO LIFE

There is no dead among the living;
There is no sick among the healthy
A lived life is a sweet life;
The twinkling star and the rising star at night
All join to offer a paean to life on earth.

Away! Away! from these arid desert lands!
Away! Away! from unknown deserts at heart!
There is no need for arid sands in watered lands;
There is no need for desert lands;
There is no need for a desert heart.

There is a need for love and care on earth;
There is a need for loving care to balm our wounds;
There is a need for a kiss of peace to mend our ways;
There is a need for light in spite of the dark;
There is a need for a smile in spite of hate.

The darkest cloud has brought the rain;
The light of the sun is seen no more;
The rose does not bloom any more;
The wren has ceased to be the king of the birds;
Day and night have parted company.

There is a need for a change of course;
This must indeed come without a bang,
But with a whimper, subdued, a glow not felt;
Love's labor is ne'er lost. *"Je vous aime!"*
There is no cloud without a silver streak.

TOUTE PAROLE EST UNE EXPLICATION
DE LA AMOUR DE DIEU

We are on fire with the sweet music of life
Our saint-like parts defy bowing to sinful life
Our souls revolt against the pains of Douleur
As we lightly sail along the sea of life
Aware of the Real Presence of God on earth.

Whatever is, is of God and from Him to us
The real essence of divine presence is hidden from us
The earth is blessed with divine Presence
Thus man is saved from dusty death
For this the thunder of Calvary roared.

Under this oaken frame the dream was born
The earth which had become the brood of men
Was conceived from time before time.
A boon of divine essences to save humanity
To take mankind beyond the reach of humanity.

Thus the history of salvation was born
The Son of God was sent to take our flesh
A loving kinosis of the Son of God
Infusing new meaning into human life.
A life without a purpose is a ship without a rudder.

Beyond this secret hiding place there is a sacred state
Of shadowed walks and canopied beauty
Of marble walls and beautiful gardens
The abode of loving tenderness and divine essence.
C'est l'etat de l'amour de mon Dieu.

PEACE

Peace is like a leaf
    Floating and rolling
    Through running stream,
    Swirling and rolling
    Like waves at bay,
    Rolling down the stream
    Down the stream of life
    In absolute tranquility
      In stillness
      And in serenity.
Peace, like a leaf, rolls with life
Unmindful of rocks and eddies.
    Rolling through tuneful winds
    And roaring boulders
    And whispering trees.
Peace brings along sweet tales
    From ocean sprays
    To you and me.
    Flowing out like a river
    To all mankind.

JOURNEY TO BETHLEHEM

It was the last and shortest leg of our journey,
We have been haunted by strange dreams, death shadows,
The storm blew strong, the tempest raged and raged,
The time was upon us to end our homeward trip,
The cold wind was blowing from the desert below
The heated sands stuck their stings in strings
As they rolled their weary ways into our noses and mouths.

We had been on the road for days and days over
Ever ready to turn back at every turn but for
Our companions, our angels and His grace
And so on and on we trekked, half exhausted, limping,
The fate of many has been determined by the stars
Of Bethlehem and there was no retiring of the Cross
Until the lovely Crown of victory was won.

His eyes have shone through the thin veil of sand
And He urged us to go on and on: "Go on, my sons!
  Go on."
His voice was almost drowned and torn by the winds
His words were like a beacon which urged us on
And soon there were no more howling winds and storms,
And no more biting sands. It was suddenly calm, serene.
I gazed and gazed in awe hoping to catch sight of Him.

And soon in spite of shifting sands I saw
Below a great void, far away, a glowing star
Beyond a village square, the object of the trek.

We drank our wine in the splendor of the lovely scene
And, like the lotus eaters, we were unable to move on
Unwilling to lose the comely moment again
The spell of day dreaming was broken, the journey ended.

Beyond my view a shining silvery light appeared
And below the foot hills were shimmering stars
A group of strangely garbed men from strange lands
Their features were equally strange, mystic, wonderful!
With leather purses filled with nuts, gold and diamonds
And marigold. Soon the baby's tiny hand
Reached out and clutched and tugged at their beards.

Now my heart on Him was fixed. "Heavens!" I said
"What can I give to the Babe of Bethlehem?
I'll trade my life for what it's worth for Him
I'll bow my head in homage to sing of Him!"
And little by little I was unable to think again.

But where thought ended and dream began I know not
Yet in the dream of death nobody returns
It was a difficult journey indeed. But I'll have it again
We trekked wearily home in a daze ready to go again
And far beyond our wildest dreams,
We crawled along the jagged mountain tops
O'er hills and dales, across ocean deeps
O'er peaceful green meadows strapped on old ruins.
And now we are home again, ready to go again.

I AM AN ALIEN

I am an alien newly stirring
From the debris of defeat,
Prying misty memories of yesteryears
Trailing the murmuring routes of evanescence
Watching my ripening nation's growth
Like evergreen luscious leaves
As its abundant rich years lie ahead
Her loveliness only tainted and ravaged
By colonial shackles and civil strife.

I am a citizen of a wide world
Crooning for a peaceful world
Seeking a place for my nation, the mighty Tree,
Strung in the wilderness
Creaking night and day in a stormy wind
Flapping its wide and feathered wings
Singing her own songs through her sons
Whose suppressed solemn songs are strong still
To bring steely sunlight to a dark world.

I am a half-heard throbbing heart
Unable to bow to the arid dust of hate
Of hateful realms lacking depths.
Amid the precipitous slopes of Time
Undulating through a maze of hills and huts
Straining the lure of sunny days
Shrinking the tinkling ripples of my heart
Shaking in the shimmering and scintillating light.
That darkens not and dims not on earth.

A DAWN

See the mighty sun heralding the Dawn
Announcing the birth of another day!
The blooming dawn reveals a distant rose
While lilies bloom like crescent lights at dusk.

The pigeon coos, the monkey gibbers in strange tunes
Which blend with the melodious music of the morn.
The spider's golden webs sparkling like gems
Break the spell of sleepless, restless night.

Thank heavens the world is not entombed
By dreary nights, nor haunted by awful dreams.
Nor encased in uncharted course of passing night.
The beautiful dawn is man's assurance for joys to come.

The sun rising from the eastern skies creates
A lovely dawn to quench man's thirst for peace;
And invites man's response to the beauty of peace.
By a perfect blend of head, heart and hand.

Away! from night's ceaseless rain and gentle storms!
Away! from the sweet, sad and dead existence!
Away! from the uneasy loss of sane acts at night!
To Dawn's merry morn and gentle winds of change.

Dawn's bright shining light makes the world seem bright,
And fills the earth with a feast of bright colors
Green, gray, yellow, orange, purple and blue
Peering through sparkling clouds lighting the earth.